BRAZIL, HOPEFULLY

#chasingsuccess

Ravi Ruparel

Acknowledgements

This book would not have been possible without the help of my family, friends, clients, employers and teachers. >> Big Hug <<

Information

Published in 2013 by 18th Day Limited

Published on CreateSpace Independent Publishing Platform

Designed by : Maciej Mraczek | typemofos.com

Typeset by: Michał Kampa | typemofos.com

Contact the publisher for all requests at:

hello@brazilhopefully.com

www.footballbraingame.com

@fb_game

All information was accurate at time of going to press.

"People want success. It's like coffee, they want instant."
— Sir Bobby Robson

"Success is no accident.
It is hard work, perseverance, learning, studying, sacrifice
and most of all, love of what you are doing or learning to do."
— Pele

About the author

Ravi studied art, economics, psychology and accounting, and has a few letters after his name to make his parents proud and his hair turn grey early. He recently turned 40. As a child he loved to breakdance and play Frogger. Ravi is a typical child from Streatham in South London, England.

Born in 1973, he has witnessed the world change dramatically. It was the year Elvis was the first entertainer to beam a worldwide telecast, the first handheld mobile call was made, Bobby Moore was captain of England, Marvin Gaye was 'getting it on' and the Vietnam War ended.

Ravi has a lovely wife, who he met at school, two lively children aged six and three (who have an ipad each) and a gorgeous cat who sadly has cancer, and will probably not make it to read this book. Today he is testing his own ability to innovate and use this experience to make his future advice and investments current and better. For now, he is a football quiz innovator. Tomorrow he resumes duty as a Chartered Accountant.

Ravi has worked for large and small companies. He helps to lead businesses through growth, financial management, change and reaching strategic goals. He has advised over one hundred businesses, all over the world, created jobs, guided entrepreneurs on how to create wealth and sparked a few people to start successful businesses, change career or do things differently. He has founded and sold his own business, helped friends grow and sell theirs and operated successfully in multiple sectors including marketing, banking, entertainment, fashion, retail and technology. He is happy when adding stuff up and making stuff happen.

Looking back, he has been a key part of teams that have created:

- £50M new revenue
- £10M of profit
- 250 new jobs
- 14 times return to investors

He likes numbers.

For Ravi, it's not about money, but about the happiness that comes from achieving success with amazing people.

One day he hopes to go to Brazil.

To Tina, Dhyan and Seva

Contents

First Half

Introducing the Chase   8

Eleven   12

The Point   14

Half Time   16

Second Half

Chasing Success   24

Ideation – creating ideas   26

Kit Bag   28

The Crowd   30

Rhythm   34

Scoring Goals   38

Hope and Glory   42

Final Analysis   43

Introducing the Chase

'The chase is the most wonderful of pastimes.'
— Numerous successful entrepreneurs

You need to understand the chase. I want to explain it to you, and why there has never been a better time to start one.

Starting a chase is by far the most important thing in building a brilliant business: a business that innovates, makes you feel good, makes money and maybe even changes the world.

I have set out the lessons learnt from over 20 years working with some incredible entrepreneurs and businesses with the story of a new, personal project to try and spark your innovation. I have refreshed myself and I want to empower you, right now!

I have been talking to my friends and family about writing a book for a very long time. Though I felt ready to share all that I have learnt, I had a feeling that the way businesses were starting and developing today, and the opportunities that exist, were different than at any point in my career. I like to practice what I preach, so I decided to wrap my past experience around a new innovative project developed with my wife, Tina, in my spare time. I did this to learn new things, confirm what I knew still held true and 'sharpen up'. I do not know if this project will be successful or not, but I am chasing and it's fun.

This project brings together different parts of my life: business, football, mobile phone apps and social media, at a moment when the world prepares for a new football season, one that will end with the greatest football competition in the world, held in Brazil, home to the world's most successful international team. This chase of mine will hopefully, virtually take me there next year, where I expect the world to change a little.

In 1500, Pedro Alvares Cabral and his fleet went in search of India and accidently found Brazil. At that point, Brazil had tribal culture that had remained virtually unchanged since the Stone Age. Today it has been through various economic and political reforms and is currently chasing democratically elected economic prosperity. It is one of the fastest growing major economies in the world, has 190 million people, abundant natural resource and one in four people is an entrepreneur. It has produced footballing legends loved the world over; Garrincha, Pele, Ronaldo, Socrates, Ronaldinho, Zico, Dunga, Kaka, Romario, Roberto Carlos and Neymar.

I believe that in 2014 football will give Brazil a spotlight , which will illuminate everything I discuss in this book. It will highlight global innovation, whether goal-line technology or real-time marketing on social media. It will also showcase a country that is undergoing change and, hopefully, showcase to the world a new set of Brazilian pioneers, innovators and football legends.

The story of chasing success has been inspired by football and a journey to Brazil. Without these two, this would be an ordinary book that you probably would not be reading right now.

Fifteen years ago, aged 25, I was working at KPMG, advising 'dotcom' start-ups across the world, and having great fun. Everyone had a business plan in his or her back pocket and everyone was a paper millionaire. Despite being a qualified Chartered Accountant and having fantastic experience, I didn't feel completely qualified to advise businesses without having run one myself.

As my colleagues went off to Manchester to get an MBA in Entrepreneurship (and before the dot com markets crashed), I decided to become one. I am impatient; I decided to start one that advised businesses. I decided to learn new things as I went along. I sold this business a few years later to work closely with leadership teams. I reduced my clients from 100 to five, practically overnight. I realised that you can't chase everything, but also, that you shouldn't put all your eggs in one basket.

Over the next few years I discovered what it felt like to chase success, day by day, as part of a management team. Most recently, I helped develop and to sell a digital agency to the largest and most successful marketing group in the world, in 2012. The agency was also one of my first clients back in 2000. Over the last three years of growth, we had mushroomed: in no time at all, we had opened businesses on three continents, won amazing clients and delivered great work. Earlier in my career I had guided a startup through venture capital funding and a stock market listing, as well as working within an equity capital markets business in swanky Mayfair during a period of exceptional profit growth.

I amicably left each opportunity at the point when my work was complete. After this latest exit, I wanted to make sure that I used my time wisely. It was the third time I had experienced success as part of a team and had previously not waited too long to jump into a new chase. I love business, helping people, chasing success, creative work, numbers and thinking.

The DNA of the chase is set out in the second half of this book. The perfect chase involves the following five factors:

1. A great idea to develop into a business model

2. Knowledge of the tools to help you work intelligently and collaboratively

3. Incentives – for everything from people to customer recruitment

4. A rhythm in your business so you can progress, every day

5. A clear vision to chase, of what the commercials and success look like

I sincerely hope I have consolidated my experiences and packaged them up here, to help you speed things up, avoid mistakes and do something awesome.

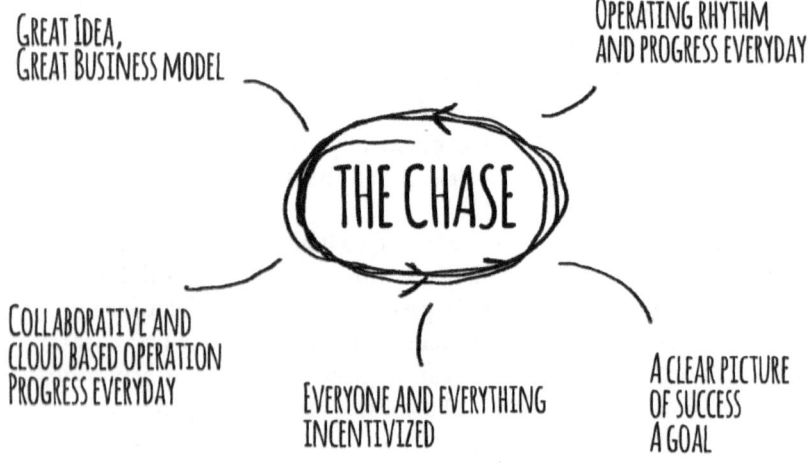

GREAT IDEA, GREAT BUSINESS MODEL

OPERATING RHYTHM AND PROGRESS EVERYDAY

THE CHASE

COLLABORATIVE AND CLOUD BASED OPERATION PROGRESS EVERYDAY

EVERYONE AND EVERYTHING INCENTIVIZED

A CLEAR PICTURE OF SUCCESS A GOAL

Why You Should Innovate, Right Now

Eleven

"The secret of getting ahead is getting started."
— Mark Twain

There are eleven reasons why I believe there has never been a better time than now to innovate and start the chase. For me, innovation is one of the key drivers of a better world. It is through the creation of new things that the world can advance in all areas: the human mind, healthcare, transportation, medicine, energy consumption, communication, arts, music, politics, justice and so on. When you combine the reasons below, they create the perfect moment for innovation and the creation of new ideas. That moment is right now, and in our lifetime I am certain we will create and observe innovation-led change on an unprecedented scale.

Throughout this book you will see these eleven reasons play out. I am dropping my pants early, and revealing the key points straight off because with 50% of books, I only read the first few chapters. I do think you should read on, because I have kept the story short and sweet. But if you don't have time, here is what you need to know about why you should get started today:

1. **Suddenly the world is connected.** The world has developed structures to allow business, words and money to travel with amazing speed. The opportunities created are huge; there are about 7 billion people in the world connected to each other. A lot of these people spend, on average, most of their days on their mobile or on Facebook, and days playing with apps. So if you add up how many times those billions of people play apps on their phone, it is, like, a bazillion gazillion. Trust me, I do numbers

2. **We are experiencing rapid evolution.** New things are created every day, in turn creating opportunities for you. I read about an 'awesome invention' or 'new idea' or something 'iconic' every single day

3. **Testing ideas is cheap.** Ideas can be conceived, designed and tested very quickly. You can do this before you invest lots of money, and potentially fail. So why not dip your toe in? You might discover you are onto something

4. **Platforms are ready.** Social networks and online conversation are waiting for you to join in and engage. People have invested a fazillion mazillion dollars to set them up for you. The same company that owns the road does not own the car. The Facebook, Twitter and Linkedin virtual worlds are ready for you and they do not innovate everything you find on them

5. **People are waiting for you.** Everyone loves something new and exciting. Go and give them a 'hug' – delight them with your innovation

6. **Developing a business is becoming cheaper and cheaper.** The cost of developing a new product, service or process has never been lower

7. **You have support for your project.** There is a lot of support for new projects. Lap it up. It ranges from free help, to tools, to meet ups and funding

8. **Now is the time for magic.** Technology suddenly surrounds us. Let's move on and make what we do with it magical. Connecting two or three things that already exist often leads to something spectacular

9. **Marketing your project is easier and cheaper.** It is more controllable and effective than ever because of digital innovation and social connections

10. **People want to play in different ways.** The way people live and work has changed. From pay as you go, to co-working, to interning and to sweat equity – embrace it all

11. **We have Brazil.** Oh yes, we have Brazil. The centre of our footballing and economic hopes. Shall we go for it? Hell yeah!

The Point

"Someone's sitting in the shade today
because someone planted a tree a long time ago."

— Warren Buffet

The point is this:

- Innovating can lead to a more rewarding life

- It can make you feel great

- It costs less than ever, so is less risky

- Someone else may do it if you don't

Innovating today gives you a way to live a different, potentially more enjoyable life. This is my definition of a better world. It has a lot more happy people, enjoying themselves and trying to reach their potential. Innovating is also easier to do, though perhaps a little scary. If you don't do it, the chances are someone else will independently create a similar idea. #ouch

Most of us sell lots of our time to somebody else. It is called work. Imagine if you didn't have to do that anymore. If you could receive money for having come up with something clever. If you worked once, and then earned again and again. That is the type of advantage that owning innovation can bring. It can also bring satisfaction, fulfilment and purpose.

The world does not stand still. It evolves. The chase is already on for many people. I see a world where we could work less and free up time to focus on moving even further forward or watching more football. Wouldn't that be nice, if we applied our time to having fun or making life better? And yes, by fun I mean football, but I also mean charity work, family time, arts, language learning, photography, looking after your young and old – the list goes on and on.

The world today presents low-cost global opportunities to create and make new products, services, processes and activities on an unprecedented scale. It seems that everyone is starting to do it. Take a leap of faith, and join a rapidly growing group of pioneers, disruptors and accountants who innovate. Yes, accountants! Remember, I am one, but for a brief moment I am going to be chasing success as a global quiz innovator. #woohoo

When you are making or running something that is your own idea, you feel different than you do in a normal job. I guess it feels the same as if you were practising a craft. I want to be an Artisan.

The feeling that you are actually making something gives you an extra spring in your step, and enough energy to move mountains. After all, if you don't make it, no one else will. Or worse – they will make it and take your moment, credit, profit and joy.

Let me tell you about the Italian mathematician Quirico Filopanti. I stumbled across him during research for my game. I plan for my game to be global and I was looking into the world clock, trying to find out what is the best time of day to host a simultaneous event in the key markets. Mr Filopanti wrote down an idea for a worldwide system of time zones in 1858 when they didn't have a proper system to organise time. The problem was, no one really read his book, and there was nowhere for him to tweet it, and no Slideshare on which to upload his power point. Worldwide time zones were calculated and organised long after he had died, but before the importance of his book was recognised. He basically invented the 24-hour clock, but no one knew! A few years after he first proposed the idea, someone else came up with the same idea in another part of the world and is credited with it. You feel for Mr Filopanti, right? Such a big idea, locked away in a little book that no one read.

The opposite scenario is this; imagine you have a gem of an idea, work hard at it and make it happen, and end up changing the world a little bit – or even a lot. You too could be like the Canadian Sir Sandford Fleming, who is credited with the 24-hour time zone. He did after all innovate this himself, he made it happen. The 24-hour clock is something that makes so much global business, travel and opportunity happen. What a great idea and quite amazing that it was only recently we have been using worldwide time zones in this way.

Half Time

"An ounce of practice is worth more than tons of preaching."
— Mahatma Gandhi

I wrote a journal of notes and thoughts while I was developing the opportunity I saw, like an unpublished blog. I was innovating to test myself again on the incubation process of starting up, learn something new and also confirm that advising to innovate right now was indeed correct. I have summarised in this chapter so you can see, through a real example, what opportunities there are.

The point of this was to go through that very difficult period of getting started. We all have an idea, we all want to be happy and successful.

But how do you move from an idea to a chase?

Today is the 14th of May 2013, and there are four hundred and twenty five days until the football competition in Brazil. My aim is to host a regular free quiz from now until on that day, based on real time football news, which everyone who has a smartphone, anywhere in the world, can play against each other. That is my big idea, and no one has tried to do it before. I want to find the biggest football brain in the world.

This is the start of my chase. Along the way, I plan to host more football quizzes than anyone ever has before. Hopefully, that means millions of questions will be asked and answered in a variety of languages. Each quiz will have the same format: 11 multiple-choice questions, 4 possible answers, available in a world where billions of people love football and have a mobile phone. Everyone likes a quiz, right? I would love you to start this journey with me. The game should be ready to launch for the new English Football season, starting on 17th August 2013. I can't wait.

What is it?

Football Brain Game is a free, 11-question real time multiple choice football news quiz which people can play against their Facebook and Twitter friends, or for points on a leader board. It is in many languages and will have hundreds of quizzes on various football topics from day one, which will be updated weekly for current football news. Players can earn achievements for fast, correct answers, or successive wins. The more correct answers they get, the higher their calculated football 'brain level' will be. The highest level a player can reach is 'legend', and they can feel like Pele or Beckham.

Why this idea?

I can't remember the exact moment I decided to create the Football Brain Game, but my reasoning process went something like this:

1. I focussed on something that had a big global and structured audience, reasoning that I would only have to capture a small share to get big customer numbers. The world, after all, has billions of people

2. I wanted to create something on mobile because everyone has one, and today most people have one of two types of operating systems (Android or iOS). That meant I would need to create only two versions. People on these phones also visit the same two shops (iTunes and Google Play); that meant I only had to get on these shelves

3. I built on something that had frequent new events or moments, so that it would not go stale or date

4. I made something contagious. Something that can be shared, liked, re-tweeted, followed and enjoyed with friends

Football ticks all the boxes and yes, I also have a passion for it. Perhaps the most telling observation I made was that everywhere I worked, football was discussed between colleagues and friends, all the time.

How big could this be?

Incredibly, football is the most watched thing on TV. Major football finals are shown in each and every country, and half of the world is reported to have tuned in to see the tournament. That is close to 3.5 billion people. It is played and watched everywhere, every week. And guess what; each of those people most likely has a mobile phone, half of them own a smart phone, and they are likely to have a Facebook and Twitter account.

Facebook was created to give people the power to share, and to make the world more open and connected. Today there are over a billion active monthly users, three quarters accessing via their mobile phone. Footballers like Ronaldo have more Facebook 'likes' (57M) than rock stars like Beyoncé (47M). Teams like Barcelona have 42 million likes. To put that in perspective – there are only 32 million people living in Canada!

Twitter is a real-time information network that connects you to the latest stories, ideas, opinions and news on your interests. During the 2013 Champions league final at Wembley, there were 4.8 million tweets about the game. At certain points in the game there were over 100,000 tweets per minute.

These platforms have really only been in place and popular now for 12 – 24 months.

So, as a rough guess at the market size for my game, I reckon that up to 50M people could want to play my game, but that could rise to a couple of billion. #jeepers

What are the risks?

I love SWOT analyses, they are a great and simple tool to 'take stock' of things. This is how mine looks today:

Strengths	Weaknesses
• Global, large audience • People love football • Nearly everyone has a mobile phone • Refreshing content to keep things fresh • Great, dynamic team	• Team based across locations and working on other things • Untested consumer product; what if no one likes it? • Revenue model requires large number of players to be lucrative
Opportunities	Threats
• Re-skin game for other products? Movies? • Physical quiz game • White label quizzes • Maybe someone will let me host his or her Corporate Box at the final? (#fingerscrossed that there is a big brand C-level reading!)	• Poor customer uptake • Technical failure • Substitute games played instead of mine • Football 'overdose' in the media • Customer drop-off during the season • England may fail to qualify? Nah...

How will I get customers?

I want to acquire customers for about £1 each. If I don't get any players, I don't pay. I love to pay for performance. Also, I should be able to target people easily and also should be able to cap my spending at, say, £5,000. I will create some brilliant, creative advertising to get people's attention. I can also display different ads to different people to see which ones people respond to. I am a fan of multi-variant A/B testing too. Basically, I'll see what works. Run one advert (A) and another (B) and follow the one people respond to. Targeted marketing can now be very efficient.

The thing about my game is this; to get the most out of it, you need to play against someone. So you need to invite your friends. I hope you invite at least 10. I hope they in turn invite 10 more. That could be 100+ people in a chain. But let's stay grounded and assume that from one person, I get 20 more. At a £5,000 spend, that means about 100,000 players. Surely they will play at least 10 of my 200+ quizzes? That's 1 million quizzes. Please help me serve up a million quizzes. The commercial challenge is to get at least 25p from each player, because then costs are covered and some.

The downer is this: in order to be contagious, I need the game to be free, free, free! No one wants to pay for a quiz and, oh, the adverts can't disrupt the game.

I need to understand the best case and worst-case scenarios in the potential outcome. In order for me to do this, I prepared the following grid. The grid analyses the potential number of players, based on two variables. These are, how many initial players are acquired, and how many friends they (and their friends, and friends of friends) introduce:

		Friends (and friends of friends) introduced per person			
		5	10	25	50
Players Acquired via Marketing	2,000	10,000	20,000	50,000	100,000
	5,000	25,000	50,000	125,000	250,000
	20,000	100,000	200,000	500,000	1,000,000

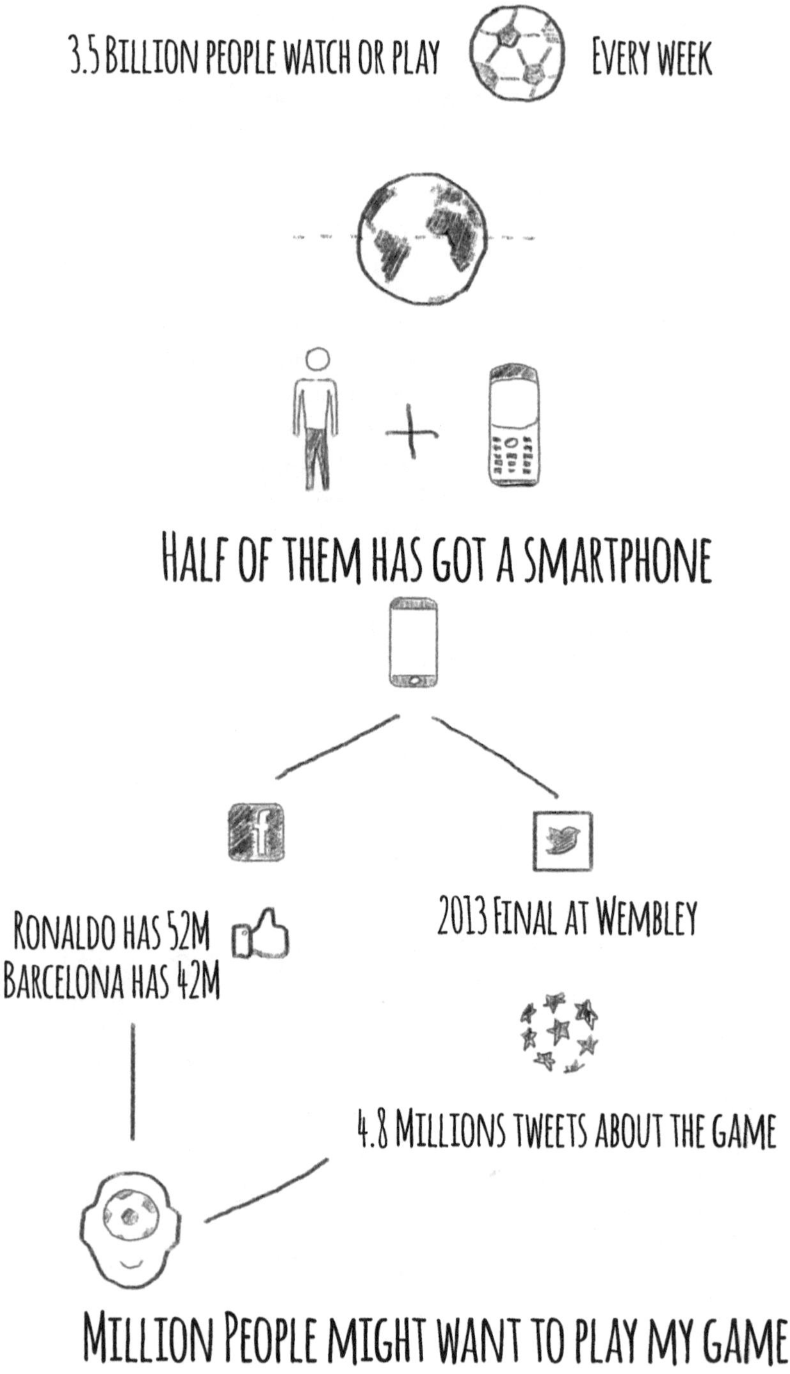

3.5 BILLION PEOPLE WATCH OR PLAY  EVERY WEEK

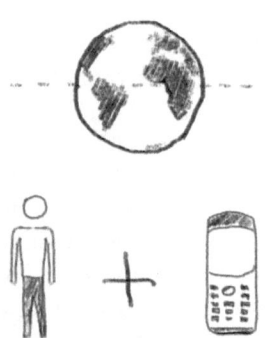

HALF OF THEM HAS GOT A SMARTPHONE

RONALDO HAS 52M
BARCELONA HAS 42M

2013 FINAL AT WEMBLEY

4.8 MILLIONS TWEETS ABOUT THE GAME

MILLION PEOPLE MIGHT WANT TO PLAY MY GAME

1 MAN INVITES 10 FRIENDS TO PLAY

EACH OF THEM INVITES ANOTHER 10

THAT'S 100+ PEOPLE IN CHAIN

My assumption is that given I have hundreds of quizzes, people will play at least 10 quizzes. This means that the worst-case scenario is I host 100,000 quizzes (2,000 people introduce 5 people and they all play 10 quizzes) and at best 10 million. #nowthatisachase

An intense 180 days...

Over a 180-day period, I took the idea through four stages of development:

1. Concept, brand and game design – these came together in a prototype and set of wire frames

2. Strategic review of commercial options, market scaling, size and structure

3. Selection of developers to build and test followed by rapid build

4. Content, partner and marketing meetings

Launching

I am now nearing the end of development and getting ready for the launch. #pressure
Everyone says it's hard to launch an app. There are so many to choose from. There are three parts to my launch plan. The main message is that I am starting a journey, a journey to find the biggest football brain in the world.

1. I plan to have a traditional PR campaign that combines this book, the innovation story of the game itself and features in this great footballing year

2. I will buy customers through online marketing

3. I will target Twitter conversation around match days, to give people special quizzes to play. This should work well on big rival days and cup games

Today is 28th July, the app store is closed, the game has some bugs, and it's raining (heavily) after several hot weeks. #life.
This is the moment before it all comes together. I would love it if you would play the game, challenge your friends and tell everyone. If you want to follow the story, please read my tweets and like my Facebook page.

In the next 90 days I will launch and you will be able to play the game and challenge your friends.

These journal entries combine, to form a clear summary of my thoughts on:

1. What this is and why I am doing it

2. How I am doing and what the risks are

3. How it will launch and big it could be

It's called Football Brain Game. Play it. It's free.

How to Chase Success, Right Now

Chasing Success

"Look at my haircut. I am ready for the war."
— Jose Mourinho

I cannot resist writing it – this is a book of two halves. Chapters 1 – 4 describe why you should innovate, together with the story of my Football Brain Game chase. The rest details the parts of the chase by combining all my experience over 20 years. Just as I expected, the experience of developing the game has given me new insight, which I will pass on, as well as made me feel a little older than I was expecting to. I am (only) 40 years old and yet when I first started proper work at UHY Hacker Young, in 1993, we had one computer between 20 people, no mobile phones and I communicated with my girlfriend via a BT pager. It is incredible how the world has changed so quickly, and it seems to be moving faster than ever. It is highly likely that your mobile, laptop, TV, games console and all your children's toys are already out of date. My kids know what Wi-Fi is but have no clue about hi-fi. Life is moving fast. The thing I do best in life is to think laterally about the development of a business, and then make it happen. Most of my experience has been working with dynamic people and game-changing business ideas with hyper growth potential. Hyper growth means any of the following that I have been lucky enough to be a part of across different businesses:

- Increasing earnings from £2M in one year to £10M the next, without adding new staff or funding

- Increasing revenue from £5M in one year to £10M, by adding two people every month to the team over the 24 month period

- Opening offices in 4 countries over a 12 month period
- Recruiting 100,000 online customers in the first few months after launching
- Selling out of a product within days of launch
- Winning awards for your work
- 500,000 YouTube views on a product demo

In each of these examples I have applied similar tactics to support the business and owners to achieve their goals. The 'formula' is fairly simple to understand and offers no guarantees, but it allows you to focus on the important things like customers, products, marketing, strategy and growth. I have often found management teams spend more time talking about how to run the business than actually running the business. Hopefully, this will speed things up for you. The chase is about how to run your business properly.

In summary, the next few chapters analyse this suggested way of developing your business:

1. Have a great idea and turn it into a business model

2. Know the tools available

3. Incentivize everything from people to customer recruitment

4. Have a rhythm in your business that allows progress, every day

5. Have a clear vision of what commercials and success look like, and chase them

I call this 'the chase' and believe it to be very powerful.

Ideation - creating ideas

"We are just an advanced breed of monkeys
on a minor planet of a very average star.
But we can understand the Universe.
That makes us something very special".

— Stephen Hawking

Every chase starts with the idea and it is by far the single most important part of innovation and business.

I'm often asked the questions "How do I come up with an idea?" and "What's the next big thing?" by people who don't know what to start up or innovate.

The brain is like a muscle. The more you use it the stronger it gets. So if you think about ideas more, I believe you will get better at coming up with ideas. I would encourage you to actively think about ideas. Make notes, draw pictures, connect two or three things and think about:

- The world

- How people spend their time and how they want to spend their time

- What they buy and sell, or want to buy and sell

- Where do they go and want to go

- Who your customer could be

- How often they would connect with you, buy from you

- The things you know about (eating, cars, hobbies, profession, fashion, music)

Ultimately, I am certain that it is because I have been thinking a lot about new things, products and ideas that I arrived at the Football Brain Game. Most natural entrepreneurs I know can formulate or analyse new business ideas in a heartbeat. So, think more and more about your context; the world you live in, and the way people live. Ideas will soon flow. As you get ideas, ask your friends and family what they think. I promise, you will soon know if it is worth going ahead. It is worth noting to share your idea but not share your business. If you have something great, people will want to be your 'co-founder'. Any co-founder that you have should be there for the full duration of the chase, and ideally complement your skills.

I am fascinated by the fact that different people see the same things in different ways, whether it's a work of art in a gallery, a penalty in football, or whether someone is beautiful or not. We are complex beings, and it is important to try to see things in different ways. This is not as easy as it may first seem, but the first step is to know that things can be seen differently.

Try and think about how someone else may view your idea: your customer, supplier, partner, friend, son or daughter.

Try and think about how someone in a different country may see things. Try and imagine how your idea would have worked five years ago or in five years' time. How could different aspects of the business change?

I know it seems very difficult to come up with a brand new idea that can change the world but it happens all the time. I have been lucky to work with some great new products like www.themu.co.uk, a folding plug that was created at the Royal College of Art and Imperial College, and www.burgopak.com, an innovative package that has sold millions and millions. Great, simple ideas both created by young minds that captured the imagination of many.

Kit Bag

"Love all, trust a few, do wrong to none."
— William Shakespeare

There is so much amazing support available, to help to make things happen. That means you can spend much less time flapping about on irrelevant things, and focus on getting an idea and making it happen. Having a stable, reliable operation to support your development and management is critical. It should just work, be cheap and deliver for you. I would like to thank the innovators behind the following collaborative tools, which are helping me to make things happen.

- Gmail, for allowing me to email the world without any fear of failure

- Easily, for letting me buy domain names

- LinkedIn, for connecting me to people who can help

- Skype, for allowing me to talk to, and message, the world

- Dropbox and Amazon, for giving me space to store, compute and share files

- Microsoft, for Excel, Word and PowerPoint for allowing me to write, add up and present

- Invision, for allowing me to prototype and showcase my game, before I had even built it

- Basecamp, for allowing me to collaborate with my team across the world

- Lynda.com for giving me video courses to learn new things

- Spotify, for playing me music I had forgotten or not yet heard

- Adobe, for Photoshop and all things design

- Unity, for allowing my games gurus to build and complete my game

- Soundcloud for sharing cool game music (and 13 Mile Charlotte for arranging the music!)

- IOS and Android platforms for allowing development

The above tools combined to allow me (for less than £200 a month) to make my quiz happen. I can talk, message and see my international team rapidly build, share, experiment and deliver the product – all while listening to everyone from the Beatles, Bob Marley, Luther Vandross, Lata Mangeshkar and even Renato Carasone. They allowed me to get to a prototype, build a minimum viable product and, in the next few weeks, to go live.

Once I launch I am looking forward to integrating with one of the new 'cloud' based packages for analytics, accounting and information reporting. In the most geeky of ways, I look forward to FLURRY, XERO, GECKOBOARD and TABLEAU.

Please use Google to discover all of these. You will love them.

The Crowd

"How you doin'?"

— Joey from Friends

My friend Justin asks everyone he meets, "What does success look like?" It is an important question and you have to know the answer. It will give you hope, and define the moment when you can celebrate. It is also OK to make the messages personal to the team member, friend or supplier. The business development team's role in the journey is to win business; the tech team's is to keep the tech systems alive and working; the support team's is to make sure business continues. Everyone has a role; together they are aiming for the same success, but their specific targets are different. I have found that incentivising people to achieve their goals creates a very healthy tension as people chase different things. This increases the chance of success, because every part of your plan is being chased by someone. It is a wonderful feeling when everyone pulls together and has hope, chasing together.

There are lots of people in your crowd who will help you. In my crowd I have strangers, friends, family and the team. They all have a special role to play. Understanding people is not an easy thing and setting people up for success is even harder. Sometimes you will misunderstand people, they will let you down, change or fail. That is human nature; it should not stop you from trying to build your team to win.

Strangers

I recommend bringing ideas to life at an early stage. One way is to design your logo, come up with the brand, and show it to your friends.

(*Please remember to protect anything like domain names, trademarks, and patents. Take professional advice, or as a minimum, Google search 'intellectual property protection' for your country.)

Meet Kirpi. Kirpi is one of more than twenty designers who entered my competition on 99 Designs for a logo. I love creating logos; I feel it brings ideas to life. We briefed 20 strangers around the world, via a website, to create a logo. We had loads of entries, some brilliant and some ridiculous. We chose Kirpi's. I think it's awesome, and we awarded him the $199 prize. Thanks Kirpi. I hope to work with you again.

Friends

I have always been independent but I've managed to surround myself with an amazing group of friends and contacts. I am grateful to have connected with people from around the world, from different industries, religions, classes and educational backgrounds. In addition to my wonderfully supportive family, I have used this support network to test the idea, and make it real. I look forward to each of them playing and telling all their friends about it.

One of the most important things I have learned in product design is that you must put yourself inside the head of your consumer, user or customer. Soon after the original idea was formed, I asked two people to help me; a creative genius (Paul) and user experience whizz (Diana). These guys came together (via the internet, as Diana lives in Krakow, Poland, and Paul in London, England) to create some serious detail exactly how a player would play the quiz. Each screen they would visit, the order of play, the special feelings they would derive during gameplay and the silky smooth navigation from the point of first contact to the point of being crowned 'legend' as a Golden 11 player. I thank these guys from the bottom of my heart, because creating experience is their craft, and they put all their love into it. I know each player will enjoy our 'beautiful game'. Once it is wildly popular (everything crossed), I will get the entire team together to see a game, and Paul will meet Diana for real.

The second important thing is to keep costs low. To do this, I set up a tender process to develop the game once it had been designed by Team Paul-and-Diana. I received quotes from Liverpool, Norway and two from Poland. After much debate, I selected an amazing group of developers from Poland – Comangle. Sylvester, Milena and Kate from Comangle are helping me to develop the game. These guys have so far been amazing. What I love is that they absolutely love games. And technology allows me to work well with them. Every day now starts with a Skype call, and ends with a reply to an update email. It works superbly. Thanks to my good friend Szczepan, I have learnt that a short flight from London takes you to Poland, where people work hard, are loyal, speak English and have a creative and positive perspective on life. I love Poland.

Family

I normally share my ideas with my wife, children, parents, sister and brother-in-law over our regular Sunday brunch. Thank you guys (Mum, Dad, Tina, Mena, Conor, Dhyan, Seva) for listening over the years, and for every future Sunday.

Team

People love new projects. They want to help, and they want to share in success. People want to be loved, and to feel talented. They want to feel empowered, to be part of a team, and to be part of a project that is great. They will increasingly work for success part-time, from home, remotely and for free. Although I would not let someone work free for me. Look after your talent. I care so much about talent development that one of my earlier ventures was a talent business, so we could make sure we got it right for ourselves. It's called Recruitmentology, if you want to go and check them out.

Looking after your talent is about being real. It is not about Fußball (tried that, didn't work), sweet bowls or suggestion boxes. It is about grown up communicating (two way), leading, empowering, teamwork and feedback. Just be honest, real and strong with your team.

#BIGHUG

Rhythm

"I give you my word that we will put in an effort. I don't know if we'll win, but we'll persist. Put on your seatbelts, because we're going to have fun."

— Pep Guardiola

Take your team on a journey they will never forget. Bring together all the parts of chasing success and give them a groove, a pulse, a rhythm. Journeys and stories have a beginning, a middle and an end. On the way, manage it all so that people get used to the direction of travel.

1. Make short-term goals with lists, and keep them simple

2. Refresh them at regular intervals (monthly, quarterly) at the same time (first Monday, third Friday) to allow your team to know the rhythm

I prefer 90-day goals. It is amazing what can happen in 90 days. Don't spend a long time analysing what went wrong or preparing your 90-day report; keep moving forward. Build momentum. Once this is in place, you can double your size, add new products, change plans or direction and people will not feel like things are out of control. With rhythm, you can be agile in the way you grow, but feel balanced and in control. Getting into a rhythm is probably the best way I have been able to help the businesses I have been involved with. Supporting that rhythm with timely business information puts the people running the business (probably you in this instance) in the best place to make the right decisions. You can't overstress the importance of routine meetings, information sharing and discussion. Each time you productively meet, you will add further value to the whole plan and goal.

I would like to illustrate the value of small, daily addition of value.

> What salary package would you prefer; £500,000 today, or a penny, doubled daily for a month (i.e., the total that results from doubling a penny daily for a month)?

The latter is over £10M. Yes, £10M. Moral? Double the value of an idea, business in rhythm and enjoy the beauty of compounding. It is possible to build incredible value.

Here are the numbers: #compounding

Day 1	0.01	Day 17	655.36
Day 2	0.02	Day 18	1,310.72
Day 3	0.04	Day 19	2,621.44
Day 4	0.08	Day 20	5,242.88
Day 5	0.16	Day 21	10,485.76
Day 6	0.32	Day 22	20,971.52
Day 7	0.64	Day 23	41,943.04
Day 8	1.28	Day 24	83,886.08
Day 9	2.56	Day 25	167,772.16
Day 10	5.12	Day 26	335,544.32
Day 11	10.24	Day 27	671,088.64
Day 12	20.48	Day 28	1,342,177.28
Day 13	40.96	Day 29	2,684,354.56
Day 14	81.92	Day 30	5,368,709.12
Day 15	163.84	Day 31	10,737,418.24
Day 16	327.68		

Part of the rhythm is to take pit stops, and take stock, regularly.

It can get quite busy when developing a business, but I always try to keep an eye on the lateral picture by doing two things on a weekly or monthly basis:

1. Make lists of 10–15 things which need doing, the important things. Sure, there is a lot of detail beneath, but it is critical to keep an eye on the big picture. A cliché? Yes, but also true

2. Support this with a traditional SWOT analysis (see chapter 4)

For me the key zone of the chase in your business is the last 90 days and the next 90 days. You should have simple, clear management information that shows you on a month-by-month basis. For example:

Key Indicator	(Past// Actual) Jan	(Past// Actual) Feb	(Past// Actual) March	(Future) April	(Future) May	(Future) June
Sales	100	120	130	150	160	200
Customers	50	55	60	70	70	75
Margin	38%	37%	37%	40%	40%	40%
New Business	80%	70%	60%	60%	50%	50%
Staff Number	6	6	7	9	9	10
Number of Visits	1000	987	1112	750	750	750
ETC	ETC	ETC	ETC	ETC	ETC	ETC

Build the key indicators around your own business, and as it grows add other important data. How did we do last year? Two quarters ago? How will we do in a year?

What is important is to set the tempo and share this among your team.

#COMPOUNDING #COUNTINGTREE

Scoring Goals

"My free-kick secret?
I just look at the net and say 'take the kick, Cristiano.'"

—Cristiano Ronaldo

Everyone loves it when someone scores a great goal (except the other team!).

On most projects the ultimate goal is to be able to make money from your idea, or at least to cover the costs – preferably quickly.

The low cost of rapid development means that in many cases you now need to make less money to cover the costs of set up and future monthly running costs. That should not matter, but it helps.

My favourite quote of all time is from Oscar Wilde, and can be repeated here to illustrate my point: "We are all in the gutter, but some of us are looking at the stars."

I take this to mean that you should keep your feet on the ground, but aim high. Do not, under any circumstance, get caught up in excitement and lose your balance as a result. I have seen too many people get carried away, and end up losing money and time.

The basic lessons for making money are straightforward:

1. Buy something for a £1 and sell it for more

2. Collect your money first, and then pay your supplier, so you are not out of pocket

3. Make sure you have an endless supply to sell

4. Include the cost of finding your customer in your calculations

5. Keep your customers happy

6. Make a simple plan for your cash flow and start to count it

If you are not sure exactly how things will pan out, don't gamble too much; test, adjust and be prepared to make big and small changes later. Alongside the idea of your business, start to consider the business model. The business model is the financial wrapper of an idea. How much would people pay? What could it cost to deliver or provide? How much could you sell?

Whilst I was studying, a teacher planted a thought in my mind that has never left me. 'On your way home Ravi, pick any business you see, like a shop or a product being advertised, and try work out how much money it makes'. I still do this on the way home from time to time. Let me give you two example of how to think.

Example 1: Italian Restaurant

I walk past an Italian restaurant and quickly observe 20 tables. I would very quickly think through the following:

-   Twenty tables of four people each

-   Seven days in a week

-   Each night the table changes three times

-   So that is 20 tables of 4, three times a night for 7 nights

-   That's 1,680 people every week

-   Every person must spend £20 at this place, in this location

-   That's £34k per week, max

-   Food must – at a quick guess – have a 50% margin? So £17k per week profit, before operating costs

-   Per annum that's £17k * 52 , £884k gross profit, max

-   Assume on average it's 50% full, so £442k

-   Rent must be £50k, eight staff at £25k each average, so say £250k per annum to run?

-   So the owner, running this really well could make £192k+. Nice.

Remember, this is just an exercise to help you think clearly. It's hypothetical and to run a place well, consistently like this is not easy. Bank managers often tell me that restaurants are tough businesses.

Example 2: Creative agency

A little shop near Oxford Street has ten staff that create designs for print. This is what I would think:

- Ten people, two must be management so not being charged to clients

- Eight people billed to clients

- They would probably be charged on average £500 per day

- They would have one month holiday, so 11 working months

- On average, 20 working days a month, 11 months equals 220 days per person

- Eight people at 220 days each is 1,760 days

- The maximum these guys could bill is 1,760 * £500 = £880,000

- They will probably achieve 70% of this £616,000

- Ten people would earn on average £40k each = £400k

- Rent and other bits probably cost £50k per annum

- This business probably makes £616k, costs £450k to run

- The owner probably makes £166k

I think like this regularly. Analysing new products, from perfume to new car launches. I really do think it helps to rattle off analyses like this, frequently. Try it.

Funding

I have traditional views on funding and financial shortfalls that you may have to make your business come to life:

1. Try to use your own financial resources to make your idea happen so you retain control

2. If you do not have sufficient funds to even get started, you should exchange equity, either to staff or investors, but still try to preferably retain control

3. Consider Crowdfunding – Google it, it's cool

4. Don't take out loans unless you are sure you can repay them, or they convert to equity on default

5. If you need to fund a timing gap between when you have to pay suppliers, and when you will receive money from customers, borrow the money, but be certain you can repay, and keep control of the cash

6. Make sure you have professional help

You should look for support from tax breaks, grants, or family and friends who may want to help you. Do not let the funding process take over your project. The 'start-up' world can become your social life, but stay grounded.

Hope and Glory

"Glory lies in the attempt to reach one's goal and not in reaching it."
— Mahatma Gandhi

My aim is to hopefully host millions of quizzes that everyone in the world with a smart phone can play, in real time, for free.

Massive, crazy dream, hey? But being part of something big, having understood the purpose, a thing that seems larger than life, is very important. I believe that you can set up a chase in your business and achieve larger success than if you don't. I hope I have shown you how in this book.

The chase is about understanding your vision, your idea and bringing together people, economics, operational rhythm, incentivise every-where and money to help you build an amazing business. You must enjoy this; it is a wonderful way to pass time. And when you reach your goal, enjoy that too.

In the next 90 days, I will have launched Football Brain Game. I hope you will connect with me and join me in a challenge. Please challenge your friends as well. What matters most is where I am going with it and where you will go with your idea.

On 22nd November 2003, I went to Sydney and watched England win the Rugby World Cup.

On 23rd August 2009, I was at the Oval to see England win the Ashes. Where will I be on 13th July 2014? Brazil, hopefully.

Final Analysis

"Some people are on the pitch! They think it's all over!"
— Kenneth Wolstenholme,
BBC Commentator 1966 FIFA World Cup Final

Eleven questions for you, as you start your chase:

1. What is the idea?

2. What does success look like?

3. Have you tested your idea on your friends, colleagues and family?

4. Are you harnessing Cloud, collaboration tools and social networks?

5. Have you got an operational rhythm?

6. Are you doing something every day to move things forward?

7. Do you have a simple commercial and financial plan, which scales up?

8. Have you thought through best and worst case scenarios?

9. Have you incentivised everything you can? People, sales, marketing, operations?

10. Does it feel like a chase?

11. Want to play?